**W9-DAD-692**

WEEKLY WR READER®

EARLY LEARNING LIBRARY

INVENTORS AND THEIR DISCOVERIES

# Thomas Edison
## and the Lightbulb

by Monica L. Rausch

**Reading consultant:** Susan Nations, M.Ed.,
author/literacy coach/consultant
in literacy development

**Science and curriculum consultant:**
Debra Voege, M.A., science and math curriculum
resource teacher

**Please visit our web site at: www.garethstevens.com**
**For a free color catalog describing Weekly Reader® Early Learning Library's list**
**of high-quality books, call 1-877-445-5824 (USA) or 1-800-387-3178 (Canada).**
**Weekly Reader® Early Learning Library's fax: (414) 336-0164.**

**Library of Congress Cataloging-in-Publication Data**

Rausch, Monica.
  Thomas Edison and the lightbulb / by Monica L. Rausch.
    p. cm. — (Inventors and their discoveries)
  Includes bibliographical references and index.
  ISBN-13: 978-0-8368-7501-0 (lib. bdg.)
  ISBN-13: 978-0-8368-7732-8 (softcover)
  1. Edison, Thomas A. (Thomas Alva), 1847-1931—Juvenile literature.  2. Inventors—
United States—Biography—Juvenile literature.  3. Electric lighting—Juvenile literature.
4. Lightbulbs—Juvenile literature.  I. Title.
  TK140.E3R38   2007
  621.3092—dc22                                                    2006029997

This edition first published in 2007 by
**Weekly Reader® Early Learning Library**
A Member of the WRC Media Family of Companies
330 West Olive Street, Suite 100
Milwaukee, WI  53212  USA

Editor: Dorothy L. Gibbs
Cover design and page layout: Kami Strunsee
Picture research: Sabrina Crewe

Picture credits: cover (main), pp. 4, 6, 8, 14, 20 The Granger Collection, New York; cover (right), title page,
pp. 5, 12 Library of Congress; pp. 7, 9 © Bettmann/Corbis; pp. 10, 13, 17, 19 © North Wind Picture Archives; p. 16
Smithsonian Institution, Neg. # 87-1732; p. 18 New Jersey State Archives, Department of State; p. 21 The Edison
Papers, Rutgers University.

Printed in the United States of America

1 2 3 4 5 6 7 8 9 10 10 09 08 07 06

# Table of Contents

**Cover:  The electric lightbulb may have been Thomas Edison's most important invention.**

**Cover and title page:  Thomas Alva Edison (1847–1931) invented more than one thousand devices in his lifetime.**

## Chapter 1
# Lights On in Menlo Park

Three thousand people gathered in Menlo Park, New Jersey. It was New Year's Eve, 1879. They heard the news about the great inventor Thomas Edison. Had he really made a useful **electric** lightbulb?

Forty lamps were on display. The people watched as the lamps turned on, then off, then on again. He did it! Edison had **invented** a low-cost, long-lasting lightbulb.

**By 1879, Thomas Edison was already a famous inventor. He was known especially for inventing the phonograph in 1877.**

phonograph

**Before electric lighting, people used candles and lamps that burned oil or gas to light their homes and streets. The candles and lamps were dirty and dangerous. They could start fires!**

Electric lights were not new to people at this time. They just were not useful. Some were too bright. They could be used only outdoors and on the streets. Others burned out too quickly.

Edison's light could be used indoors. It lasted a long time without burning out, and it did not cost very much to make. It made light by heating a very thin piece of material.

**Edison's very first lightbulb used electricity to heat a thin piece of cotton thread.**

# Chapter 2
# A Bright Boy

Thomas Alva Edison was born on February 11, 1847, in Milan, Ohio. When he was growing up, Edison was always asking questions. He wanted to know how everything worked.

Edison did not do well in school. He could not hear very well. When he could not hear the teacher, he did not pay attention. The teacher thought he could not learn, but Edison's mother knew he was very smart. She began to teach him at home. Edison also spent time at the library. He read lots and lots of books.

At the age of thirteen, Edison worked on the **Grand Trunk Railroad**, selling candy and newspapers to passengers. He ran a **laboratory** and a printing press in the train's baggage car.

When Edison was very young, one of his biggest interests was the **telegraph**. When he was about fifteen, he saved a telegraph worker's son from being hit by a train. The worker was very happy. He offered to teach Edison how to use a telegraph.

**Telegraph workers had to know Morse Code to send and receive messages.**

By age sixteen, Edison had a job as a telegraph worker.
He wanted to know everything about the telegraph.
He studied it while he worked. Soon, he was inventing
things that made the telegraph work better.

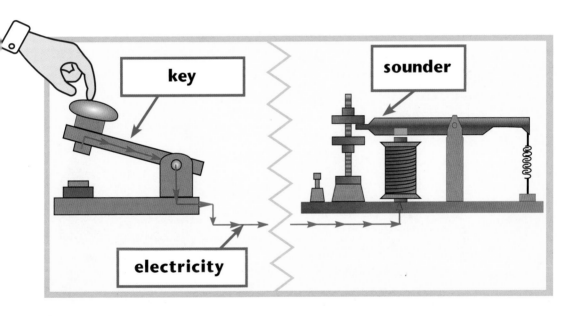

A telegraph machine sends messages from a **key** to a **sounder**
through an electric wire. A worker uses the key to tap out
a message in Morse Code. Another worker receives the
message by listening to the sounder and changes the code
back into words.

Edison invented a machine that could print telegraph messages.  He sold the idea for this machine to a company.  The company wanted to make the machine.  Edison sold other ideas, too.  He used the money he made to invent new things.

**Edison's home in Menlo Park had an office, a laboratory, and a machine shop.  People worked there, making inventions.  Edison was the first person to pay a large group of people to work as inventors.**

In 1877, Edison tried to find a way to **record** telegraph messages. He did not do it, but he did discover how to record voices and play them back. He invented a machine for recording and playing back sound. He called the machine a phonograph.

Edison's first phonograph had a sharp tool that made marks on tinfoil to record sound. Another tool could read the marks to play the sound. Edison improved his phonograph many times. This model used wax tubes instead of tinfoil.

# Chapter 3
# A Bright Idea

Many of Edison's inventions used electricity. Edison was very interested in electricity. He wanted to learn about electric lighting, too. He knew that other inventors were making electric lights, but no one could find a way to make one that lasted a long time.

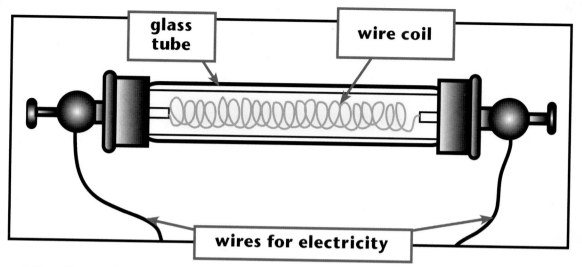

glass tube

wire coil

wires for electricity

The first electric light was invented in 1820. The light had a coil of very thin **platinum** wire inside a glass tube. Electricity heated the wire to make it glow. The light worked, but the platinum metal needed to make it cost too much.

Edison thought he could make a better electric light. He knew that to make a lightbulb last a long time, the electricity had to pass through a very, very thin piece of material. The electricity had to heat the material to make it light up.

The material Edison needed had to heat up without burning up and falling apart. He wanted the light from the material to last a long time. Air made the material fall apart faster, so Edison needed to find a way to take the air out of the lightbulb. He discovered he could use a **vacuum pump**. Now he was getting close!

vacuum pump

Edison improved a vacuum pump invented by Heinrich Geissler and Hermann Sprengel in 1875 to take the air out of his first lightbulb. In 1929, Edison and a man who worked with him at Menlo Park showed how they used the vacuum pump back in 1879.

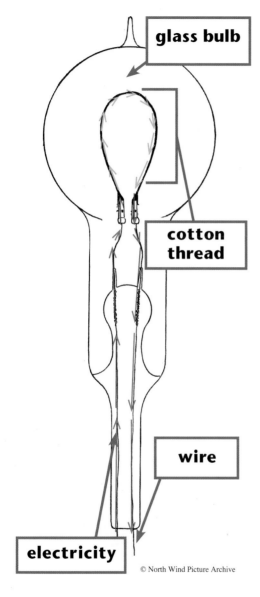

**glass bulb**

**cotton thread**

**wire**

**electricity**

Edison pumped the air out of a glass bulb. Then he put a piece of cotton thread inside the bulb. Next, he ran electricity into the bulb. As the electricity passed through the cotton thread, the thread lighted up. It stayed lit for more than thirteen hours! Edison had invented the first long-lasting lightbulb.

**Normally, a thin piece of cotton thread will burn up very quickly. Inside a glass bulb without any air, the same piece of cotton thread will burn much longer.**

17

Now Edison wanted to find materials that made the light last even longer. He tried six thousand different kinds of materials. The materials came from plants. He used pieces of plants from all over the world! Japanese **bamboo** lasted the longest. In January 1880, Edison used bamboo to make a lightbulb. The light lasted about twelve hundred hours!

**This picture shows three of Edison's early lightbulbs. The lightbulb he invented in 1879 is on the right. The improved bamboo lightbulb is on the left.**

Bamboo filament lamp     Manufactured lamp at Menlo     First successfull lamp

**Edison opened an electric lighting station in New York City in 1882. It was the first electric power station in the world.**

While he was making lightbulbs, Edison also found a way to get electricity into people's homes. People needed electricity in their homes to use lightbulbs. The electricity came from a **power station**.

# Chapter 4
# City Lights

In 1879, Edison set up forty lamps in Menlo Park, New Jersey. He wanted to show people that he had made a good electric lightbulb. People were amazed. They began to call Edison "The Wizard of Menlo Park."

Edison's first power station, in New York City, lit up 1 square mile (2.6 square kilometers). It made electric lights possible in many homes. More and more people wanted light!

**Thomas Alva Edison died on October 18, 1931. Three days after he died, many people in the United States turned off their lights for one minute to honor this great inventor.**

# Hoover Suggests "Minute Of Darkness" as Nation's Homage to Thomas A. Edison

PRESIDENT Hoover issued a statement in Washington yesterday suggesting that all individuals in the United States extinguish their lights for one minute tonight as a tribute to the memory of Thomas A. Edison. The President set 10 p. m. as the moment for the tribute in Eastern Standard Time. The President's statement read:

"The grief of every American in the passing of one of the great benefactors of humanity has manifested itself in the suggestion from hundreds of citizens that the nation should join in a solemn tribute to the memory of Thomas Alva Edison.

"In response to this universal desire to pay personal respect to Mr. Edison's memory, I suggest that all individuals should extinguish their lights for one minute on Wednesday evening, October 21, at 7 o'clock, Pacific time, 8 o'clock, Mountain time, 9 o'clock, Central time, and 10 o'clock, Eastern time. It is my understanding that broadcasting companies will undertake a brief program in respect to Mr. Edison's memory at this moment.

"The suggestion had been made that the electrical current at generating plants should be turned off at these hours, but on inquiry I find (and this is confirmed by Thomas Edison, Jr.) that this would constitute a great peril to life throughout the country because of the many services dependent upon electrical power in protection from fire, the operation of water supply, sanitation, elevators, operations in hospitals and the vast number of activities which, if halted even for an instant, would result in death somewhere in the country. It is not, therefore, advisable. This demonstration of the dependence of the country upon electrical current for its life and health is in itself a monument to Mr. Edison's genius."

# Glossary

**bamboo** — a type of strong, lightweight wood

**coil** — a set of rings or loops, turning one after another, in material such as wire

**invented** — found a new way of doing something or made a new tool to perform a task

**laboratory** — a place where scientists and inventors test new ideas

**material** — anything that can be felt when it is touched

**Morse Code** — a pattern of short and long bursts of electricity, known as dots and dashes, that stand for letters of the alphabet

**phonograph** — a machine on which recorded sounds are played

**platinum** — a valuable grayish-white metal

**power station** — a place where electricity is made

**record** — (v) to copy sound on some kind of material in a way that the sound can be played back for a listener to hear

**telegraph** — a machine that uses wires and electricity to send messages over long distances

**vacuum pump** — a machine that can suck all the air out of a closed-in space

# Books

*A Picture Book of Thomas Alva Edison.* David A. Adler (Holiday House)

*Thomas Edison.* Compass Point Early Biographies (series).
  Lucia Raatma (Compass Point Books)

*Thomas Edison.* First Biographies (series). Lola M. Schaefer
  (Capstone Press)

*Thomas Edison: Inventor.* Famous Inventors (series). Carin T. Ford
  (Enslow Elementary)

*Young Thomas Edison.* Michael Dooling (Holiday House)

# Web Site

Edison Invents!
*invention.smithsonian.org/centerpieces/edison/*
Play Edison Invents! and learn about Thomas Edison's life
and inventions.

**Publisher's note to educators and parents:** Our editors have carefully
reviewed this Web site to ensure that it is suitable for children. Many Web
sites change frequently, however, and we cannot guarantee that a site's future
contents will continue to meet our high standards of quality and educational
value. Be advised that children should be closely supervised whenever they
access the Internet.

# Index

# About the Author

**Monica L. Rausch** has a master's degree in creative writing from the University of Wisconsin–Milwaukee, where she is currently teaching composition, literature, and creative writing.  Monica likes to write fiction, but she says sticking to the facts is fun, too. Monica lives in Milwaukee near her six nieces and nephews, to whom she loves to read books.